Contemplations and Undertones

Katamneni Gopichand

ISBN
Hardcase 979-8-89777-675-7
Paperback 979-8-89699-525-8

A tribute to my beloved father Mr. K.S. Rao

&

Dedicated

To my Mom Ms. K.B. N

My wife, my daughters Divya & Snigdha, my son Deva

All my teachers especially Ms. Mariamma, Ms. Anjali Dhar &
Ms. Usharani.

My beloved Brother Mr. K. Gopi, Sister Ms. K. Madhavi &
Brother-in-law Mr. Vimal,

My Doctor Mr. P. Saikumar, my friends, near & dear ones.

Mr & Mrs. T. Jayapal Reddy, Directors - St. Peter's Institutes

Contents

Personal Growth & Self-Reflection

Self-discovery and Inner Strength

Nature, Work & Virtue

In Nature, Work, and Virtue

SPECIAL POEMS – PHILOSOPHY

Existence, Truth, and Beyond

Technology & Communication

Connections in the Digital Age

Preface

This anthology of poems, drawn from diverse facets of human experience, offers a profound exploration of the many threads that connect us: society, love, personal growth, nature, technology, and philosophical musings on our place in the universe.

The poems are organised into six distinct groups, each offering a lens through which we can examine the complexities of the world around us. The first group, *A Society's Struggle*, delves into the deeper issues that define our collective existence—justice, inequality, corruption, and the scars left behind by war and power. It challenges us to question the systems that govern us and exhorts us to seek a more equitable and compassionate world.

In *The Journey of Relationships*, we explore the bonds that define us as human beings. These poems celebrate the eternal nature of love, the strength and beauty of womanhood, the nurturing presence of mothers and fathers, and the guidance of those who teach us. The complexities of these relationships are explored with honesty and tenderness, urging us to reflect on the connections we hold dear.

Personal Growth & Self-Reflection takes us inward, inviting us to examine the very core of our being. From the importance of skills that shape our identity to the power of gratitude, hope, and communication, these poems remind us that the journey toward self-awareness and inner strength is one of constant evolution and discovery.

In *Nature, Work & Virtue,* the poems celebrate the virtues of hard work and dedication found in both nature and human labour. Whether it is the farmer's toil, the corporate world's relentless pursuit of goals, or the cultivation of virtues in our personal lives, we are reminded of the interconnectedness of work, nature, and character.

The *Special Poems – Philosophy* group takes a step beyond the tangible, questioning the very essence of existence. Who owns the universe? What is the true measure of reality? What illusions do we carry with us as truths? These philosophical poems encourage us to look beyond the surface and explore the metaphysical dimensions of life.

Finally, *Technology & Communication* brings us into the modern age, where our lives are shaped by digital tools and the constant flow of information. From artificial intelligence to the devices that connect us, these poems highlight the duality of technology—as a force for connection, but also as a force that demands our attention and reflection.

This book is not just a collection of verses; it is an invitation—an invitation to question, reflect, and grow. It challenges us to ponder the most fundamental aspects of our existence, from the personal to the societal, from the fleeting to the eternal. As you read, take your time. Let the words guide you to a deeper understanding of yourself, others, and the world we inhabit.

I hope that, like the characters in these poems, you will find moments of reflection, growth, and connection that will stay with you long after the pages have turned.

Introduction

In an age where the world often pulls us in a thousand different directions, Contemplations & Undertones serves as a quiet yet powerful call for introspection and authenticity. This remarkable collection of poems offers more than just verses; it is a guide for navigating the complexities of life with clarity, truth, and purpose. With each carefully crafted piece, the author invites readers, particularly the younger generation, to reconnect with the timeless values of morality, ethics, and integrity. Through poignant reflections on society, relationships, emotions, and philosophy, the poems transcend mere observation, offering profound lessons on how to live with authenticity and serve both oneself and the broader community.

What sets this collection apart is its interactive nature, providing readers with the opportunity to become participants in the creative process. The inclusion of poems with open-ended stanzas encourages readers to fill in the blanks, edit verses, and explore their own voice, transforming the act of reading into a personal journey of self-expression. In this novel approach, each reader becomes both poet and scholar, discovering their own truths and resonating with the depth of meaning in each line. Moreover, the collection contrasts traditional and modern versions of the same poem, offering an insightful exploration of cultural shifts and the ways in which timeless ideas evolve.

Contemplations & Undertones is an exploration of thought, emotion, and creativity—blending depth with engagement in a seamless harmony.

Every poem offers a distinct sense, a unique message, and an opportunity for transformation. It challenges us to pause, reflect, and navigate the intricate layers of life with purpose and authenticity. This volume is a call to remain true to oneself, to avoid the distractions of an ever-changing world, and to serve not only one's personal aspirations but also the greater good of family and society.

This is not just a collection of poems; it is a journey, an invitation to explore the nuances of life, to shape one's own narrative, and to live a life guided by wisdom, ethics, and unwavering truth. It is a poetic journey for those seeking both depth and engagement, and above all, for those who are ready to reflect on what truly matters.

A Society's Struggle

Justice, Power and Truth

Echoes of Inequality
Torn between two worlds

Poor are those

who dwell in slums,

in slums dumped with waste,

where shadows loom,

their homes found in lumps of gloom,

no swimming pools unlike the rich,

just cesspools bare,

Injustice weighs in the stagnant air.

* * *

World torn into two,

the rich and the poor, the silence hums,

And the truth reveals,

there's even something more.

The rich, they thrive on labour's toil,

their lavish buildings & castles

built on costliest lands,

For the rich

the wealth paints the score,

For the poor

the hunger demands much more.

* * *

The poor....

Build bridges strong,

their achievements untold,

They bear the weight of the world's NEGLECT,

Yet in their iron hearts,

dreams deep hidden but never unfold.

For every brick arranged

with blistered hands,

they craft the future of this world,

proving their worth,

The poor are the silent architects,

Work under the blazing sun

to earn a piece of bun,

a humble wage.

* * *

Beneath the sun's relentless glare,

the poor toil on,

in silent prayer,

On life's stage

the rich are the poor,

the poor are the rich,

it's the poor who make

the rich, richer and richest.

Though they lack material gain,

their resilience shall forever reign.

* * *

Poor are those, in nature's grasp,

stand so meek,

they are born to embrace change.

The seasons and times may peak,

a gust might pour a basket

of dust into their huts

with no doors and windows to close,

and extreme winters, they froze.

* * *

Heavy rains may pour,

they prepare their minds…

as if habited at seashore,

feeling the waves

to crash and ebb away,

they know, the darkest night

is followed by the dawn

to drive away the darkness.

And if the dawn is not bright,

they accept they were not right,

keep their fingers crossed tight'

waiting for the light & warmth.

* * *

Steadfast, the soul of the poor stands tall,

A lighthouse burning bright

through storms that call.

In every season, through wind and rain,

Their strength remains unshaken

And in the darkest hours, it shines bright,

guiding the lost & craving souls with unwavering light.

Corruption
The subduction

For a few among many, corruption, not just a mission but

the sole vision,

its creation, ensuring the pervasion, is all a game of plan.

Seeds of greed, planted deep, the required feed,

Fostering a culture where common and innocent bleed.

Intent to damage the society's DNA, causing the mutations,

Corruption, the cancer, it spreads without cessation,

acquired and inherited.

Honest labourers toil like bees, their hard-earned nectar

Stored in hives, stolen by thieves,

The poor remain poor in corruption, they bend &

the few' grow richer in corruption, for they amend.

* * *

Corruption with new tricks, it clicks,

Integrity wanes, corruption filled in veins,

The poor and the middle class trapped in the cycle

of destitution, bending under the weight of

corruption's oppression.

Laws are enforced, legal actions strict,

But difficult to restrict,

the roots deep since generations old.

Tall claims to eliminate this sinister,

Unfortunately, politicians, the true magicians' adept at

weaving illusions of progress, reality always a distress.

* * *

Systemic reforms deployed from time to time,

the legal measures, to address the root causes of corruption &

its treasures, effectiveness lack as those few escape with a knack.

Spread across in every field, their influence and

Expertise does stack, society's values erode,

element of trust corrodes.

From politics to business, and beyond, corruption's

Shadow casts its bond, forms many

a twisted liaison, and sowing discord along

its treacherous path.

* * *

Corruption, not just a volcano, to be seen as eruption,

It is the unseen disruption, the SUBDUCTION,

Every nation's value melted down

and descending deeper and deeper.

It is an invisible and invincible ghost

leaving a trail of decay and distrust in its wake,

Nation's progress is at stake.

The day is not far from leaving behind

a trail of darkness,

Yet still we ignore in our blindness,

It thrives on our silence, forevermore.

Oh, hush now all, in silence tread,

Silent, silent, silent as the silence of the dead.

TAXES

"Burdened Hearts, Call to Justice"

A tax for this, a tax for that,

The weight of burdens growing fat.

The common man, with weary stride,

Feels the yoke of taxes, wide and wide.

Each coin, each fee, a silent cry,

A plea that echoes to the sky.

Yet hear me, Government, hear me well—

For every charge, there's a tale to tell.

We know the need, we know the call,

To fund the state and serve us all.

But in this world of endless cost,

The common soul should not be lost.

* * *

Do not, dear leaders, blind and cold,

Lay every weight upon the bold.

The worker's hands, the dreamer's mind,

Are not made to be chained and confined.

Let not the poor be driven to woe,

While the rich, untouched, continue to grow.

A fairer hand, a gentler touch,

Can spread the load, can ease so much.

For we, the many, who toil and care,

Deserve to breathe, deserve to share.

Take what's needed, but with some grace,

Let not your burden fall on one's face.

* * *

At the hotel door, at the station line,

We pay our dues, yet long for time.

But freedom's worth, and peace of mind,

Cannot be sold or left behind.

Let not the cost-of-living rise,

To dim the light behind our eyes.

For taxes come, as taxes go,

But still, the heart must freely flow.

So, gather your share, collect your due,

But let it be just, fair, and true.

In every step, in every breath,

We strive for life, not for death.

No toll can claim our inner light,

The government must take its part,

But not at the cost of people's heart.

For, in the end, we all shall see,

The strength of unity, and liberty.

So take what's fair, but let it be,

A tax that builds, not one that bleeds.

For the common man, for every hand,

We seek a world where we can stand.

Together, free, with hearts that shine,

A future built on what's divine.

When the common man must travel far,

From humble home to city's star,

He finds the price for every ride,

A mountain high, a rising tide.

A flight, a train, a bus, a taxi,

Each one, it seems, demands a fee so tax-y.

To journey forth, to meet the need.

* * *

He must starve, for the costs exceed

What little he has earned today—

The road's a toll he cannot pay.

For every seat, for every mile,

He must pay in hunger, in pain, and in trial.

Let the government take what it must,

But may it never break our trust.

A fare for this, a fee for that,

No room for breathing, no space for fat.

* * *

The Government's hand, a grasp so tight,

Turns a man's day to endless plight.

With every step, with every stride,

The cost of travel swells with pride.

The price of freedom, in each fare,

Makes the traveller's soul despair.

The riches flow,

but the poor are drained,

By policies that leave them chained.

The common man, a desperate plea,

To journey free, to live and be.

* * *

So let the Government hear this cry,

And know that we cannot just comply.

Fair taxes are the cost we pay,

But let us not be led astray.

The traveller's toll should not be life,

It must not come at such a price.

For taxes come, as taxes go,

But still, the heart must freely flow.

So gather your share, collect your due,

But let it be just, fair, and true.

In every step, in every breath,

We strive for life, not for death.

So, take what's fair, but let it be,

A tax that builds, not one that bleeds.

For the common man, for every hand,

We seek a world where we can stand.

Together, free, with hearts that shine,

A future built on what's divine.

Let the Government take what it must,

But may it never break our trust.

The people's strength, the people's will,

Can never be taken, can never be stilled.

47

"Scars of War: The Ruins of Humanity"

"Torn hearts & Broken lands - sorrow in the wake of destruction."

In the heart of humanity, *war* always leaves a scar,

The scar etched deep, its presence some Nations love to keep,

Rivalry amongst nations with feelings of hatred & aggression,

Massive artillery & tombs of bombs for destruction.

War's fury unfurls, a relentless flow,

HUMANITY, no more to survive and glow,

Relationships killed and buried, chances scarce to pair,

Attempts futile to repair, giving up in despair.

Wars' devastation reigns, across every inch of land,

Years of hard work undone, by its merciless hand,

Basking in the glory of nationalism, the only aim…

LOSE YOUR KIN TO WIN,

Madness so much, nothing comes to mind,

NO sadness in committing sin.

In the pursuit of power and domination,

the humanity's essence wanes,

cities bombarded,

leaving behind blood-soaked terrains,

Hearts are torn asunder,

yet no realisation of human blunder,

Nothing prevails, no brotherhood, no motherhood…

ONLY FALSEHOOD.

The echoes of laughter and joy, perish

and replaced by cries,

Amidst horror and terror beneath war's crimson skies,

no lessons learned from past,

where devastation did sow, aghast,

wealth spent, Nations proud of stealth,

destroying nature's health.

Many children, the young and the old,

In war's *RELENTLESS DANCE OF DEATH*, they fall,

Families torn apart &

victims left to answer its call.

Targets chosen to smash,

buildings burnt to ash, still opinions clash,

Humanity left behind in uncertainty,

nature left with ecological backlash.

Madness speaks louder than reason or love,

To conquer, to claim, without thought of the cost—

In the end, what is gained, when all is lost?

Election
The wrong selection

Election, truly a grand affair,
No entry for many aspirants who are fair.
Power always vested with the highest chair,
Yet hope persists for change to declare.

The politicians and leaders of parties speak,
Poor voters, with empty stomachs and roofs that leak,
Mutual allegations among rivals unfold,
Yet truth always untold.

The politicians,

their promises so tall and grand,

Yet for the poor,

reality is a piece of barren land.

Poor voters, in every election,

they hope to retrieve,

But find themselves forgotten,

struggling to believe.

Election rallies

with many stories of deceit,

Truth never in the nearest sight.

Poor voters,

unable to question the might,

No strength to rise, to join the fight.

Politicians cheat through tweet,

The lies told so sweet,

false promises repeat.

Poor voters,

on the brink of defeat,

Amidst the chaos,

the trust deplete.

While elections,

on the political stage,

The poor voter for his presence,

is paid a day's wage.

The technique of every politician

to harness the voter,

Like a butcher preparing for slaughter.

Many politicians,

adept authors of fiction,

Crafted with eloquent diction

"power" their addiction,

Masters of manipulation

and rich in action,

Deserve an Oscar for their perfection.

Amidst the sea of noise,

poor voter,

stands alone with no voice.

In the game of politics,

truth's obsolete,

The unfair practices repeat,

Nation's dreams incomplete.

Politicians,

the election stage's magicians,

With sleight of hand

and clever incisions,

They weave their spells

casting illusions,

Crafting promises and creating confusions.

In the theatre of votes and election's screen,

they take the centre stage,

With practical skills

and smiles, they engage,

The common man,

he always believes,

In the tricks, these politicians conceive.

The poor voters,

not to repeat the errors,

Holding their leaders to account,

with clear mirror,

Must realise, with the show over

and the lights dim,

their votes must be cast such that

the reality not to appear grim.

So let not the illusions be the heart's guide,

But the promise of change, honest and wide,

For when the election's stage is set and done,

The TRUE POWER lies in the VOTE OF ONE.

"The Liquid Truth"

Drink, drink and drink,…..

The glass in your hand begins to clink,

With every sip, you start to think,

Of moments shared, of bonds you link,

But beware, for too much can make you sink.

Drink, drink and drink,…..

Up to brink, values shrink,

As the night wears on, the line grows thin & thin,

The once firm morals slowly begin to spin,

What was once right may seem a sin.

Your mind's a blur, your vision beams,

But you still believe you're chasing dreams.

Yet all you are chasing is the last cocktail's gleam.

Drink, drink and drink,…..

Now you're the expert, an alcohol sage,

Spinning tales from a long-lost age,

Order the toast & you start to boast,

With confidence high, you raise your glass,

Tales of glory, love and past,

Laughter echoes, as moments pass,

But a slurred word reveals the contrast.

Friends surrender...

for they make you the king to pay the bill,

they laugh, they cheer, they toast and fill,

their glasses high, hearts all still,

Yet, when it comes time to settle the thrill,

It's you who'll pay the bill, at will.

The Journey of Relationships

Love, Bonds and Growth

"Eternal Vow"
"A Love Beyond Farewell"

Eternal is my love for you

A bond of affection and care, tightly woven,

Even the faintest glimmer cannot elude its embrace,

Such is the hold of my love.

My heart has been a voyager true,

Seeks you alone, its journey through,

Softly it murmurs, "I am Not yours, but Hers",

A truth that my soul tenderly stirs.

In nature's haven, where whispers trace,

Each sip of wine, a reminder of your grace,

The moon, the stars, in celestial frame,

Proclaim that you are divine, my eternal flame.

Whispers of the breeze, gentle and near,

Assuring me, "Our love will endure, for it is pure"

Yet, let you not be a distant star,

For in your light, my hopes align, not afar.

My soul roams, wandering free,

Across vast lands and endless sea,

Seeking the haven of the greatest ship,

The sanctuary of our relationship.

In your presence, every breath finds its rhythm,

A melody of love, sweet and solemn,

With each inhale, your fragrance I sense,

Exhaling gratitude for your enduring grace.

Our love spans the breadth of my being,

Filling every corner, every feeling,

In your arms, I find solace and peace,

Again, a sanctuary where all worries cease.

Feelings stirred, like waves upon the shore,

Longing for your presence, forever more,

In your arms, my soul finds its core,

A love so deep, it leaves me craving more.

In your eyes, I see my reflection,

A soul entwined in our affection,

In you, I find my purpose, my guide,

With you, I'll journey side by side,

With each heartbeat, your name resounds,

Echoing in the chambers where love abounds.

I'll live for you, with every breath I take,

In your love, I find everything,

In sleep and in thoughts awake,

In every triumph and moment of fame.

And if fate decides our final farewell,

I'll embrace it boldly, in love's sacred spell,

"For your love is eternal, my heart's only desire."

The Radiance of Womanhood

She wakes long before sunrise

Ere the cock's crow…

With no alarms shrill, no bells ring,

Her spirit rises.

With the morning's first hues,

In her embrace of responsibilities vast,

She serves with selflessness unsurpassed,

Yet never does she bid her kin to

Clear their dues,

Her love's currency, a bond that forever ensues.

No measure to value her service,

She is truly family's treasure,

Her pressure, she keeps away

And fills herself with joy and pleasure.

She takes the blame many times,

Yet staunch as steady flame.

She doesn't take harsh reactions to heart,

FOR *YEARS LONG*,

She has mastered the art.

She bears barbs, her moods high and low,

Like tides of a relentless sea,

She knows her role is unique,

No cravings for promotion or recognition,

She bears everything for the family,

Her dedication lies in unwavering devotion.

She encourages everyone in the family,

Keeps herself empty without any expectations,

For she strives ever for the relations,

She is a silent force of strength and grace,

Her heart so big to give everyone an equal place.

Father

Oh, my dear Father,

When I was a boy, you were my finest toy,

Every moment wrapped in laughter,

all around was joy & joy,

You were my first friend,

our adventures, games and fun, knew no end,

In your warm embrace, I found my strength,

You were my rock, my mentor & supporter,

Oh, my dear Father,

You were the captain of our ship, guiding our place,

The whales and the sharks …

could not shake our sturdy craft,

With wisdom and strength,

you navigated each draft.

Through turbulent waters,

you steered us with care,

In the chaos of life,

you showed us how to dare.

Oh, my dear Father,

As I grew older,

you gifted us responsibilities,

In the pursuit of our dreams, you set us free.

You handed us the compass,

showed us how to chart,

But in that act of love,

it broke my young heart.

You minimised your burdens,

took to a smaller boat,

While I sailed on,

I never thought you'd float,

Past me like a stranger,

drifting out of sight,

I screamed out "Ahoy, Ahoy" in the fading light.

Now, I realise, dear father,

that life is a fleeting fad,

Moments-like whispers,

both joyous and sad,

In life's journey,

your love weaves my soul,

Each lesson and each laugh

made our family whole.

Oh, my dear Father,

I remember our voyages,

the tales that we spun,

The stars that we chased,

the races we have run,

The years may pass,

and seasons may change,

Your blessings surround me, in every small range.

You sacrificed so much for our happiness,

Now I understand,

the weights you have lifted,

And all the valuable things you've gifted.

Father, I know you are tired,

and it's time to rest,

But now I stand alone

in this life's vast quest,

The forest, I must find my way,

With your love as my guide,

I'll face each new day.

Though you've sailed beyond the horizon,

out of my view,

Your love is the anchor,

steadfast and pure.

In every challenge that I face,

I hear your voice so nearby,

Guiding me gently, calming my fear.

So, here's to you, father,

my captain, my guide,

In the ocean of memories,

you'll always reside.

Though the winds may change,

and the tides may shift,

Your love is invaluable,

my most treasured gift,

In every kind gesture,

in laughter and light,

Your spirit shines on,

a lighthouse so bright standing tall,

With each step I take, I honour your name,

In the ocean of love, we'll always remain.

Mother
Oh, my dear Mother,

Oh, my dear Mother, forever your child,

You gave me birth, a gift so true,

Your womb, a warm cradle, a safe place to grow,

The umbilical cord, our first bond, you know.

I don't know how many times
I was to die in the womb,
Yet you never turned it to a tomb.
Instead, you breathed life into me,
time and again.
A silent guardian,
through each uncertain strain.

You were both a doctor and God,

a healer divine,

And I can't grasp the depth of the pain that was mine.

Mom, I don't know what struggles you faced,

To keep me alive in that sacred space.

How much you gave, how much you bore,

All for me, your child, the one you adore.

Though, I can't remember those early days,

I felt your love, in so many ways.

You raised me with kindness, always nearby,

A shield against hunger, a comforting sigh.

I never knew thirst,

you quenched every need,

With gentle hands,

you planted each seed of character.

You taught me respect,

and how to stand tall,

Filled me with courage,

you gave it all.

Your love was balanced,

so fair and so bright,

If I could measure it,

it would fill up in the night.

More than any number,

it's precious and rare,

A treasure beyond what any Math could declare.

Oh, my dear Mother,

Your eyes see me deeply,

more than a scan,

You are my best doctor, who understands.

You are my best friend,

my closest ally,

In laughter and tears,

together we fly.

You are my angel,

my guide on this road,

In all of life's trials,

you lessen my load.

You are my counsellor,

wise and sincere,

With every word spoken,

I hold you so dear.

You are my teacher,

with lessons taught so clear,

In the school of life,

you calm every fear.

You are my coach,

cheering me on,

In every small victory and win,

your spirit lives on.

Oh, my dear Mother,

Your sacrifices are many,

your strength always shows,

You carried my burdens,

through highs and lows,

But, dear mother, forgive me if I'VE lost my way,

I promise to be there, every day.

In your love & blessings,

my worries all fade.

Every day was a festival,

bright and alive,

With you by my side,

I learned how to thrive.

Every sweet you prepared,

each dish made with care,

I long to be childlike,

to feel love in the air.

The honey of your affection,

sweeter than the rest,

Today, I have riches,

but your love is the best.

Oh, my dear Mother,

My mother, with you,

nothing could ever sway,

In the heart of our home,

love finds its way,

Forever your child,

with gratitude, I stand,

In the warmth of your love,

I find life so grand.

But now, I plead with all my soul,

my heart laid bare,

Give me a chance,

a chance to serve you, to care.

To be as your father,

in love and devotion true,

This is the only way I can repay all that's due.

For all you've given,

for all you've endured,

Let me give back, your love reassured.

And to all sons and daughters,

heed this call,

Love your mother, for she gave her all.

Teacher
My guide

"Yes, I have a bright future," I declare with might,

My faith in my teachers shows me the light,

With knowledge as compass and virtue as oar,

I sail toward horizons, unknown shores in-store.

With patience and care, they nurtured my mind,

Opening doors to a future so brilliantly designed.

Through their words, I learned to soar,

To dream, to believe, and to strive for more.

"Yes, I have a bright future," with each step I take,
Grateful for my teachers, whose wisdom I awake.
In their lessons, I find strength to aspire,
For they have kindled the fire of my desire.

"Yes, I have a bright future," in the halls

of my mind, their voices echoes,

their invaluable teachings to borrow & grow,

I step into the future, with strength for tomorrow.

Yes, in this world of competition, I stand,

With roots anchored deep in knowledge's grand.

For here, amidst beauty and growth so abundant,

I find the strength to be truly confident.

"Yes, I have a bright future," I whisper in awe,
With my teachers' guidance, I rise without flaw.
With their encouragement, I break through barriers tall,
My belief in them, will not allow me to fall.

Through the corridors of time, their voices ring,

Their guidance sustains me, like flowing streams.

With the lessons ingrained, I chase my dreams,

In their legacy, my future beams.

In their guidance, I've found my way,

I have laid my road to greatness, day by day.

Every lesson taught, rich with wisdom,

Yes, my teachers, made me the one

to grow & glow in freedom.

Their lessons are seeds

that blossomed within,

Guiding me forward,

beyond where I've been.

In their light, I've become

all I'm meant to be,

A reflection of their love and wisdom,

Marriage – Life's Carriage

Marriage, a journey we started long ago,

Sailing through time, steady and slow.

I, your quiet strength, you, my heart,

Together we've walked, never far apart.

We've seen the seasons come and go,

Through sunny days and winds that blow.

In laughter and tears, we found our way,

Side by side, day after day.

The children we raised, like seeds we planted,

Nurtured with love, and sometimes chanted.

They grew, they learned, and took flight,

Carrying with them the love we ignited.

Love's not always easy,

we know that well,

But through it all, with trust... the guide,

We've weathered the storms, with nothing to hide.

The years have rusted some of our dreams,

But still, we hold on to what it means.

In every wrinkle, in every grey,

There's a promise we made, and it still holds sway.

We've learned that it's not about the grand,

It's in the little moments, hand in hand.

Through joys and struggles, through calm and strife,

We've shared this beautiful thing called life.

So here we are, still walking strong,

With memories to carry, and hearts that belong.

In the quiet of dawn, or the warmth of the night,

We rest in each other, our love still alight,

Our souls bound tight.

Marriage
A plea to the younger generations

Marriage is not just a word,

But a relationship filled with promises and vows,

It's the life that one likes to build, the love that allows.

It's not just exchange of rings or grand display,

For bride, a SACRED BAND

throughout her life – HUSBAND

And for bridegroom, A LIFE forever – WIFE.

It's the person you lean on, through thick and thin,

The one who sees your soul within.

Marriage isn't perfect, no flawless design,

But it's the way two hearts become one.

It's the growth that happens, year by year,

The learning to love….

For in each other, the purpose is clear

It's the patient healing when wounds are deep,

And the promise you make, to always keep.

It's not about perfection, nor endless bliss,

But the quiet contentment in trust.

The purpose of marriage, in truth,

Is to walk through life with someone

whom you have owned.

It's a partnership built on trust and respect,

Where each person finds their own special place.

It's not the destination, it is the journey.

Yet in today's world, where love seems to wane,

Marriage is often seen as a fleeting gain.

The younger hearts chase a fleeting thrill,

Seeking change, but never standing still.

They wonder, "Why bind yourself for life?"

When there's always another, and no end to strife.

But what if we saw marriage for what it could be?

A sanctuary of trust, where hearts fly free.

Not a cage to trap, but a space to grow,

Where love deepens with each day passed.

It is the union of two souls, not merely to endure,

But remain as inseparable, in a symphony pure.

For the real value of marriage isn't just the start,

It's in the patience, the progress, and the prosperity.

Personal Growth & Self-Reflection

Self-discovery and Inner Strength

Skill - the Permanent Seal

Skill says, I am your distinct seal,

none can steal,

With dedication and effort,

months, or years of practice

You have earned my embrace,

Forms many, but with you I am,

for you have chosen a path,

Through trials and triumphs,

you've carved out your space,

As God belongs to everyone, so do I,

I am not for one alone but for all.

Certainly, I love the one who has worked hard,

committed and pledged for knowledge.

I am divine,

In you' I am to make you shine,

In you' I am to make you survive,

& In you' I am to make you revive.

Your Natural parents give you a name,

I am the one to give you the fame,

So, cherish me well, and in your achievement,

my brilliance will shine.

Let me speak about who I am in each one of you

In the pulse of your hands, a healer's touch

In your steady hands, I find my beat.

With each entry posted, in financial precision,

Through numbers and balance, I set the vision.

In the log of wood, I take my form,

I am the flawlessness sculpted with grace.

Through the pipes, I am the coursing tide,

In every fix, every overflow, I remain the steady flow.

In the courtroom's drama, I take the stand,

In your defence, I am the righteous strand.

In the heat of pans, I come alive,

A culinary art, where Flavours meet, I am the feast complete.

In the strokes of brush, I am the creative drive.

I come alive, with every shade & blend, in your masterpiece.

In the current's flow, I am the flame,

In illumination, I am the guiding light.

In the roar of engines, I find my might,

With every nut & bolt and through every fix.

In the soil's deep hold, I take my root,

In your garden, I am the fruit.

In blueprints laid, I am the design,

Structures rising where dreams align.

In your constructions, I am the grand design.

In the mind's deep space, my purpose unfolds,

Through every session, each conversation and test,

In healing hearts, I am the gentle rest.

In languages spoken, I bridge the gap,

In your translations, I am the linguistic map.

Braving infernos, where dangers sprawl, I find my call,

With each rescue, every trial, I am the unyielding wall.

In the threads you weave, I am the stitch,

Fashioning garments where styles enrich.

In the tunes you play, I find my tone,

With every chord and every key, I am the harmony.

In the lens focus, I capture the light,

With every shot and every click, I am the perfect sight.

In your narratives & stories, I find my tale

In your writings, I am the literary trail.

In the race you run, in every space,

I keep my pace, I am the relentless grace.

In the climb of hill,

I am the power of your will; I am the might.

In the waters, I take my dive,

In your swimming, I am the aquatic thrive.

On the green expanse, I find my swing,

In your golfing, I am the king.

On the winding road, I find my ride,

In your cycling, I am the relentless glide.

On the ice's gleam, I take my spin,

In your skating, I am the icy win.

In the skies' expanse, I find my flight,

In your innovations, I am the aerospace delight.

On the stage spotlight, I find my role,

in your performances, I am the theatrical goal.

In the sphere of pixels, With every click and every gain,

In your marketing, I am the digital lane.

In the sea of data, I find my insight,

Analysing trends where numbers ignite,

In your analysis, I am the digital light.

In the arena of threats, I find my shield
Protecting networks, where dangers yield,
In your defence, I am the digital seal.

In the world of content, I find my voice,
In your creations, I am the digital poise.

Oh all, so heed my call, both far and wide,

let effort and hard work be your guide,

Awake with the power of skill,

And success is always on your side.

Simplicity
The Greatest City

The city that remains silent,

Yet it glows.

The city that doesn't make noise,

Yet remains poise.

The city that doesn't show off

Yet wins the show.

The city that doesn't boast its glory

Yet stands glorified.

The biggest city ever

But built by own.

The city that stands gold

Though it is old.

The city that faces adversity

Yet remains to be a university.

The city, with no ambience

Yet known for its silence.

The city that doesn't chase fame,

Yet everyone knows its name.

The city, a quiet storm,

Whose calmness is its form.

The city that builds dreams,

Without a word or sound.

The city blessed with inner light,

Yet rules with silent might.

The city that moves with quiet stride,

Yet fills the world with pride.

It is the city of the heart,

A puzzle none can solve,

Where the less it shows, the more it speaks—

A mystery to evolve.

Self-Defeat
—A Path to Rise

Fear to perform a feat,

To take the chance, to feel the heat,

Shivers wrap the feet,

Lacking confidence to bet,

Hesitant to work hard and sweat.

Prefer to quit,

Claims oneself a misfit.

Doesn't dare to grit,

Prefers to be in comfort,

A preferred fort.

You prefer to lose,

For your thoughts are loose.

It is the path you choose,

You prefer to be tied up within a noose.

Want to wear a winner's hat,

BUT within you, a Cat.

Want to march toward the success,

but within you, a coward.

Want to reach high,

But shy,

Doesn't want to see the light,

Your plight, no flight.

No signs of hope,

You're tied up with a rope.

No strategies to cope with,

Within you, the extremes,

The NORTH and the SOUTH.

No decision—caught in the midst,

Lost between the dream and the mist.

The fear is a shadow that haunts the mind,

You seek the answers, but none you find.

A heart that trembles at the chance to rise,

Too caught up in the webs of lies.

The lies you tell, not to others, but to you,

That you can't succeed, that you'll never break through.

Yet, the heart that weeps within the chest,

Knows deep down it's yearning for rest,

Not in comfort, not in the easy place,

But in the struggle, in the race.

For it's in the fire that metals are forged,

In the storm that the soul is enlarged.

The fear is but a cloak you wear,

Hiding the warrior beneath the despair.

The winner within is locked,

Afraid to fight & win.

But courage, it lies dormant within,

Waiting for the battle to begin.

Still, you cling to the soft and warm,

Shying away from life's true form.

You call yourself a misfit,

But you are not broken, not unfit.

The world is vast, with paths untold,

If you'd only let go, you'd be bold.

For every misstep, every fall,

Is just a part of the rise, after all.

The winners weren't born with perfect grace,

They stumbled, they failed, but they embraced the race.

The winner's hat is not given by fate,

It's earned through every step you take.

Yes, you want to win, to take the crown,

But you're still sitting, weighed down.

The path is steep, the climb is high,

But what's a life if you never try?

The greatest joys come from the fight,

Not from hiding away in the night.

Want to soar, to touch the skies,

But you're bound by fear and silent cries.

Your wings are clipped by doubt and shame,

You run from the risk, you hide from the flame.

But the flame is what lights the way,

It's the spark that guides you through the grey.

You long to reach, to rise above,

But you're shackled by the weight of love—

Not for others, but for the comfort zone,

Where you live, yet never truly own.

The fire inside, you must ignite,

If you ever want to touch the light.

The rope that ties, the chains that bind,

Are of your own making, of your own mind.

The extremes within, they pull you apart,

One side whispers hope, the other, "Don't start."

But deep down, you know what's true,

The only one holding you back is you.

If you dare to step beyond the line,

You'll see the stars begin to shine.

If you dare to take that leap,

You'll break free from the fears that creep.

And when you rise, you will be strong,

For you'll have found where you belong.

No more excuses, no more doubt,

The courage to act will cast it out.

You're not a misfit, not a fool,

You're just afraid to break the rule.

The rule that says, "Stay small, stay safe,"

But the true path is for the brave.

Your strength is waiting, deep inside,

Waiting for you to take that stride.

The self-defeat you've come to know,

Is nothing but the fear to grow.

Break free from it, let it go,

And you will find your inner glow.

The rope will loosen, the noose will fade,

And you will see the progress you've made.

For the winner's hat is never far,

It's within you, it's who you are.

So, step into the light, embrace the fight,

Climb the mountain with all your might.

For in the struggle, you'll find your worth,

And finally, step into your rebirth.

The "______" Chained

Reason for Blank: The blank can be filled with ego or addictions like smoking, alcoholism, procrastination, complacency, gossip, etc. Multiple poems can be derived from this one poem and the reader can customize it accordingly with the stanzas.

Oh, my dear __________

Your hold on me knows no end,

I can't live without your tight embrace,

For you, my love, I'll keep the chase.

I claim you as my precious prize,

Ignoring all other's heartfelt cries,

I don't need their voices, their plea,

When I'm wrapped in your spree.

You love me so much, it's true,

For in your clutches, I remain askew,

You never leave no matter what,

You are always there, in my thought and gut.

Oh, my dear ____________

Your love, it smothers,

Holds me tighter than any others.

For in your grip, I'm not truly free,

Just a puppet dancing your decree.

You are ubiquitous, it's true,

In every heart, every mind, you brew,

There isn't anywhere that you are not there,

A constant presence, beyond compare.

In every thought, you take control,

You are so special always; with you, I roll.

Your hold relentless, your grip unyielding,

You are my constant companion, always concealing,

In the darkness, you shine so bright,

Revealing the vanity, blinding my sight.

You are everywhere, in every space,

Your hold has an unyielding grip,

Beyond your grasp, true freedom lies,

But I pray that your presence never dies.

Oh ____________ you are a cunning foe,

A companion I can't seem to let go,

Your presence, a burden I bear,

Yet in your grip, I'm forever chained.

Your whispers fuel the fire inside,

A false strength, a swelling tide,

You promise power, control, and might,

And trap me deeper in the plight.

Your praises blind, your doubts confound,
In your shadow, I'm tightly bound,
After every fall, I rise once more,
Still clinging to your deadly lore.

Oh __________ your chains, they shine so bright,

You bind me tight with those chains,

Yet steal my calm, you blind my view.

The truth, still you "Shine"…

Gratitude

Gratitude is the key to relationships,

A virtue of morality.

An appreciation for oneself and others,

It teaches us to see the good,

To lead a meaningful life,

A life where happiness is a choice.

Happiness is the path to gratitude—

Not found in riches or fleeting moments,

But in the simple joys, we often miss.

Gratitude for life,

For nature's wonders,

For peace,

For kindness and love,

For blessings that come in many forms.

Gratitude for self and others,

For the help we give and receive,

For opportunities that arise,

For generosity,

For forgiveness,

For time—both present and future.

Gratitude for parents,

For their endless love and sacrifice,

Their selfless support & comforting embrace.

Gratitude for teachers,

For opening minds to knowledge and growth,

For their patience and dedication,

For shaping our futures with care,

And inspiring us to strive for more.

Gratitude for doctors,

For their healing hands and kind hearts,

For their expertise and compassion,

And bringing comfort in times of need.

Gratitude for blessings,

For the moments of grace we receive,

For the little miracles that surround us,

Creating the hope that sustains our minds and spirits.

Gratitude for siblings,

For shared memories and childhood bonds,

For the laughter and love that lasts,

And for the relationship that never weakens.

Gratitude for children,

For the joy they bring into our lives,

For their innocence and boundless love,

For their curiosity and wonder,

For reminding us to cherish every moment.

Gratitude for friends,

For their loyalty and understanding,

For being there through thick and thin,

And for the warmth of their companionship.

Gratitude for spouses,

For love that grows and deepens,

For the partnership and shared dreams,

For supporting each other's journey, walking side by side.

In all these forms, gratitude blooms,

In every heart, it lights the way,

Filling us with joy,

Filling us with peace,

A transformative force,

That shapes our world and guides us forward.

Realisation of self and society

Is the gateway to deep gratitude.

A heart full of appreciation,

An attitude that transforms—

It shapes us, and shapes the world.

The Hope
The invisible rope

The heart, an ocean of many streams,

VAST AND DEEP, shattered dreams,

Love & joy IN SILENT SLEEP,

Anger's fire and jealousy's bite,

Fear that grips, sorrow that falls,

situations' silent calls.

Frustration's howl, envy's sting,

Yet amidst this swirling tide,

What is it that dares to guide?

The hope, an invisible rope,

Gives you life when you grope.

A flicker in the deepest dark,

It fuels the soul, ignites a spark.

From first to last, it stands as light,

A force that drives through day and night.

It tells you that success is near,

while dispels the fear.

It lets you sail, no matter how wild,

Turning adversity into opportunity, reconciled.

But hope is not just for the here and now,

NOT WITH JUST WITHIN YOU AND ME!

It stretches far beyond the present,

A vision for those who have yet to appear.

It speaks not only to the heart of today,

But to future hands that will find their way.

A guiding light for those yet unborn,

A promise of dawn after every storm.

Hope weaves through time, its thread so fine,

A bond that links us to the divine.

For in the seeds we plant and the paths we chart,

the legacy we leave behind,

Will guide the generations yet to find.

It is the hope for a world still to be,

Where love and peace are all we see.

A future shaped by hands of care,

A world where all hearts are free to share.

In every act, in every prayer,

Hope builds the future, strong and fair.

"*Eli, Teach Me to Speak*"
Oh Eli, I want to speak,

But I can't.

People say I am an introvert,

I carry many inhibitions,

A silent world where I often drown,

Yet, I long to find my voice, to rise above the crowd.

Let me know, my friend, how to catch the flow,

I stumble and fall, I am slow,

And in the quiet of my heart, I feel low,

But there is a fire inside that wants to grow.

Help me, dear friend, to sow the seeds,

To cultivate my words,

Give me the tips, the keys,

To unlock the door, to breathe, to speak freely.

Eli, her friend, gently smiles,

And speaks of the art that spans the miles—

The art of communication is simple, she says,

Whether introvert or extrovert, we all have our ways.

A message, a thought, a dream to share,

It's just the courage to let go of the fear.

To simplify it, my dear, she explains,

Speech is a garland, with no constraints,

Each word, a flower, blooming bright,

The thread is the heart, holding them tight.

And in the space between, you will find,

The beauty of connection, the peace of mind.

My friend, you must sow the seeds,

Nurture them slowly, with care and grace,

Let them grow at their own pace.

For the journey is not about haste,

But about patience, and knowing your place.

Raise and nurture the plant, she says,

Water it with your thoughts and praise.

Let the words stretch, let them climb,

Into the sunlight, out of the grime.

And soon you'll find, with gentle ease,

The words will come, like a cool, fresh breeze.

So speak, my friend, speak with pride,

No need to hide, let your heart decide.

For in each spoken word you'll see,

The blossoming of your soul, set free.

Nature, Work & Virtue

In Nature, Work and Virtue

Farmer - The Real Hero

The farmer, my hero, noble and true,

With seeds in hands, the future's sown,

In his fields, our futures breed,

For he serves his purpose with valiant deed,

With dawn's first light, he greets the day.

The farmer, my hero, noble and true,

With a ray of hope and with nature's clue,

Greets the day to enter the fields with plough,

He tills the soil, his sweat endow.

The farmer, my hero, noble and true,

Spends seasons through, in fields so wide,

In him, nature's grace and strength abide,

In every seed sown, his dreams reside.

The farmer, my hero, noble and true,

Known for the efforts he invests,

Sometimes not a match that he harvests,

With pests that devour, his patience put to test.

The farmer, my hero, noble and true,

His hopes grow in each row he tends,

Though sometimes nature becomes harsh,

He stands tall and refuses to yield,

His determination, an unbreakable shield,

A true warrior on the field.

The Corporate Honeybee

In the garden of business, the corporates bloom,

Each corporate a flower, adorned with allure,

Lures employees, the bees with the fragrance,

Seemingly sweet and pure,

Neither the flower nor the bee is sure,

Uncertainties endure,

For in this garden of ambition and strife,

The rules are dynamic, ever-changing and alive.

In the garden of business, not alone they stand,

Not all find the nectar, to call their own,

Few gather the nectar, with a careful advance,

Crafting their legacy in the game of chance.

Some wither away, their dreams overthrown,

In the cycle of growth, they remain unknown.

Oh, the flowers may wither, the bees may stray,

But in the garden, new life finds its way.

For in each struggle, each challenge met,

Lies the wisdom of paths we must not forget.

And though some dreams may fail to rise,

The garden lives on beneath the skies—

Ever-changing, ever-growing, ever true,

In its embrace, the bees old and new are all born anew.

The Garden of Virtues

In the realm of your struggle, a silent applause rises,

For the good you plant, in soil unseen, reaps its prize.

The wave of your heart, calm or tempestuous,

Bears the truth of your being, radiant or restless.

Anger, like a storm, clouds the open sky,

But in its shadow, you lose your way and sigh.

Jealousy, like thorns, pricks the tender flesh,

While greed binds the soul, in a knot, a silent mesh.

Procrastination lingers, like the setting sun,

Leaving only frustration when the day is done.

To compare oneself with another's flight,

Is to forget the light that blooms in your own sight.

Patience, a bridge built over time's river,

Brings forth the fruits of labour, and a heart that quivers.

Hard work, humble and pure, a golden thread,

Woven through the fabric of the dreams we are fed.

In every effort, a treasure is found,

The commitment, like roots, deep in the ground.

Punctuality is the morning's first light,

While knowledge brings the dawn, pure and bright.

In wisdom, a kingdom, where freedom takes flight,

The service of life, the eternal thesis of night.

A heart of fortitude, steadfast and true,

Love, the dove, soars in skies of blue.

Truthfulness, like youth in its bloom,

With accountability, a soul's true room.

Discipline, the breath that keeps the flame,

And intellect, the whisper that calls your name.

Mindfulness, the silence that speaks,

In stillness, kindness grows, where peace peaks.

Purpose, like a tree, bears fruit unseen,

Its roots deep in the soil of what has been.

Desire, like fire, burns bright and high,

And the cravings of the soul, like winds, rush by.

On the path of spirit, there is no afterthought,

Only the now, where the self is sought.

In meditation's gaze, the world is renewed,

A revelation of elevation, where hearts are subdued.

Collaboration, the dance of souls,

Building foundations where celebration unfolds.

The goals we seek, like distant hills,

Mark the journey, where ambition fills.

Wishes bloom, like flowers kissed by rain,

Dreams flow gently, like streams unchained.

Needs, like roots, stretch deep within,

While wants, like towers, rise in the din.

Comforts, like the soft earth, cradle the soul,

And luxuries, like stars, glitter, making us whole.

Your experiences, like the tides, teach,

The lessons of life, beyond what we can reach.

The path of your journey, a song so sweet,

Celebrates the joys where the heart and spirit meet.

Your status, a blend of what you choose to be,

Shaped by the journey, like waves on the sea.

Values, the reflection of the soul's pure light,

Achievements, like echoes, in the endless night.

Gratitude, the source of endless bliss,

A beacon that guides through moments we miss.

Your feelings, tender leaves in the wind,

Blossom anew, where all things begin.

The Garden of Virtues
Reflections (a profound view) & Higher impact

I see you, fighting with fire, bold and brave,

Your actions, like thunder, shake the ground,

Your good deeds—seeds scattered wide—

Tear through the soil of the world and grow.

What are your emotions? Waves that crash and roar,

Anger, a tempest, but it drags you down—

Feel it, yes, but let it not drown your soul.

Jealousy? A weight that shackles your flight—

Free yourself, soar, be bold and rejoice.

Procrastinate not! For the world waits for no man,

Time, relentless, pulls you toward the unknown.

Comparison? Forget it! Stand tall in your own skin,

There is no one like you in the endless expanse!

Delayed gratification, a gift to those who endure.

The work, the sweat, the call of labour—

This is your treasure, this is your glory.

Effort—yes, it is the currency of your life,

It's the worth you've earned, not given.

Commitment—solid as the ground beneath your feet,

A promise to the self, to the world.

Punctuality, a rhythm that beats with the pulse of the earth,

And knowledge—the song of the mind,

Endless, boundless, a joy beyond measure.

Wisdom—the crown of your journey,

You wear it proudly, a beacon for all to see.

In your service, I see the path to greatness,

Not in titles or crowns, but in your deeds.

Your fortitude? The rock that holds you firm,

Your love? A flame, a beacon, a force that unites.

Truth—raw, pure, and unyielding—

Let it flood your being, wash you clean.

Accountability, the mirror you hold to your soul,

Discipline—the anchor to which you tether your dreams.

Mindfulness—oh, how stillness speaks!

In quiet, your kindness ripples out.

Purpose, yes, it roots you deep,

Bringing forth fruits in the fullness of time.

Desires? They burn bright, sparks in the night sky,

But let them not consume you, let them guide you.

The spiritual path? It clears the way,

A light that never flickers, only shines.

Collaboration—the strength in numbers,

Together, we build, we rise, we celebrate!

Goals—each one a star, each one a dream,

Each one a step, marching toward the future.

Wishes, like winds, sweep through the plains,

And dreams, they flow like rivers to the sea.

Needs—roots that bind us to the earth,

Wants—clouds that float, ever-changing, ever free.

Comforts? Yes, they cradle you, they ease your bones,

But it is the struggle that shapes the man,
The luxuries, fleeting as the winds,
Yet they spark joy, like sunlight on the horizon.
Experience? The map that guides you,
Each step a mark, each trial a lesson.
The path you walk—forever unfolding—
It is life itself, this is the road to the soul's jubilation.
Your status? It is what you make of it—
A reflection of your choices, your heart's true will.
Your values - they are your voice in the world,
Your achievements, the mark you leave behind.
Gratitude - the sunlight that bathes the land,
It fills you, it overflows, it gives you strength.
Feelings? Yes, tender, true—
They rise and fall like waves on the shore,
But they are yours, the spring that waters your soul.

Special Poems - Philosophy

Existence, Truth, and Beyond

Who Owns the Universe

Vast… beyond the reach of thought,
A cosmic ocean, so profound,
A verse or multiverse, some ask,
Yet none can fathom, none can grasp.
Unending by length, breadth, or depth,
A labyrinth of mysteries wrapped,
The fabric stitched by unseen hands,
Beyond the gaze of human lands.

Who owns the stars, the deepened sky,

The boundless void where comets fly?

Who owns the quarks that spin and twirl,

In quantum dance, a hidden world?

Not just the Earth, or moonlit beams,

Not just the rivers, trees, and streams.

The answer hides in places dark,

In empty space, in every spark.

What are we, if not stardust born?

A speck, a whisper, here and gone,

A fleeting breath within a tide,

A pulse of life, a short-lived ride.

The atoms that make up our form,

From distant stars, they once were torn,

And in our cells, they whisper still,

Of ancient time, of cosmic will.

Molecules that bond and break,

Are fragments of a grand mistake,

Or are they threads in woven strands,

The weaving done by unseen hands?

What of the bonds that hold us fast,

In love, in hate, from first to last?

Do they extend beyond the skin,

To other worlds we've never been?

The particles, the sub-particles,

Spin in realms both strange and radical,

Invisible paths that twist and turn,

At speeds where space and time will burn.

Beyond the naked eye's pursuit,

The universe plays its quiet lute,

Unseen, unheard, unmeasured still,

It dances to a higher will.

And yet we search, we strive, we seek,

For answers that remain mystique.

The solar system, the Milky Way,

The planets that in silence sway,

The moons, the stars, the distant light,

The galaxies that hide from sight,

Each a verse in an endless song,

A choir singing all night long.

What if gravity had never been?

What if no force held us within?

Would we drift through endless space,

Without a point, without a place?

Would the universe unfold in grace,

Or scatter, shattered, through time and space?

A thought, a question, ever pure,

Of laws we cannot yet ensure.

Magnetism, the hidden force,

Guides the universe along its course,

Unseen hands that pull, that push,

A symphony in every hush.

The dance of atoms, the pulse of stars,

The universe is mapped in scars,

Each one a story, each one a clue,

Of all we knew.

Nature, the creator, moves unseen,

Through fractals vast, through spaces green,

In mountains tall and oceans deep,

In promises, we fail to keep.

It whispers through the breeze and rain,

In quiet joy and deepened pain,

In nature's laws, in each heartbeat,

In every step, our lives repeat.

And yet, we are more than dust and stone,

More than atoms, all alone.

We glimpse the mystery, we seek the truth,

In shadows long, in forgotten youth.

For the universe is not a verse,

But a multiverse, beyond the spiritual immerse,

A boundless plane, a timeless sea,

Where none can own, where none are free.

God's manifestation, some would say,

A hand that shapes the night and day,

A force that bends, a will that guides,

That spans the cosmos, far and wide.

But who can say where gods reside,

In stars so far, in oceans wide?

Beyond science, beyond all thought,

The universe leaves us overwrought.

For it does not answer the deep quest,

It holds no mercy, no sweet rest.

Beyond the bounds of reason's grasp,

It leaves us with a silent gasp.

The mysteries grow, they never cease,

As we wander through them, seeking peace.

And in this vast, unmeasured space,

Where time and matter interlace,

Where stars are born and planets die,

Where moons in orbit slowly fly,

We ask ourselves, with eyes that burn:

Who owns this universe, this turn?

The stars, the sky, the darkened sea—

Is it not the same as you and me?

We live as sojourners in this room,

Called Earth, a cradle for our doom,

A fleeting moment, a whisper loud,

Beneath the ever-rolling cloud.

We build, we break, we fight, we cry,

We seek the truth, yet pass it by.

Wars for land, for greed, for gold,

Fights for power, wars retold.

Yet what are we, when all is lost?

When time reveals the true cost?

Do we remember that we are small,

That all is fleeting, none can call,

This world their own, for long to stay,

That we are but a breath, a day?

Why fight, why quarrel, why divide,

When none of us can here reside?

We quarrel over dirt and stone,

Over places we do not own,

Forget the stars, forget the sky,

Forget the depth of why, oh why?

We are passers-by, guests at best,

In this grand house, a fleeting quest.

And one day, soon, the door will close,

And in the silence, no one knows.

Who owns this vast, unending land?

The stars above, the grains of sand ?

Who owns the dance of time and space?

The forces that we can't embrace?

Maybe the truth is not for us to find,

Maybe we are the ones who are blind.

For in this universe, so wild, so free,

We live as tenants, but we fail to see.

The true owner is not man or sky,

Not the stars that burn so high,

Not the forces that bend and twist,

But something far beyond our list.

Perhaps, it's not to own, but to live,

To love, to learn, to give, to give.

In this vast cosmos, forever wide,

We are just pieces of the tide.

So ask yourself, when life seems grim:

Who owns the light, the dark, the hymn?

In the silence, in the space,

In the grand and endless race,

We are but dust, yet in that dust,

We live, we dream, we rise, we trust.

For we are sojourners in this space.

The True Measure – Real State

Oh, for what you are proud…
You have been here with nothing,
With nothing, but the air YOU BORROWED to breathe,
Whatsoever, it is, it simply is…
For after the role you've played, you will exit,
And claim nothing as your own.
When the "I" in you is
Not yours, then what is yours?

THE TRUTH, the Presidents of most

Powerful nations are not permanent residents,

THE SIMPLE NUANCE to understand

EVERYONE ON THIS STAGE IS IMPERMANENT.

The riches you own, the luxuries you enjoy

Nothing is yours,

The names you carve in stone,

They are left alone.

The real state is *NOT THE REAL ESTATE*,

The measure is not the square feet earned, nor the costliest fleet,

It is finally the small quiet place of 6 OR 7 feet

where you will be laid to rest.

You may claim a GRANDEST Mansion,

In the end, the greatest Mansion is the GRAVE,

The place same for MASTER & SLAVE,

We are all equal in the dust.

What remains, then, is not the gold or the throne,

But the legacy of kindness you've sown—

The love you've spread, the hands you've reached,

The hearts you've touched, the lives you've freed.

For, in the end, it's not what you've owned,

But how you've loved, how you've made hearts your home.

With time, the names may fade,

But in love and service, life remains eternal.

Illusions

Within the chambers of the mind,

Within the depths of the heart,

He sits enthroned, to make the strongest falter,

He bends the brave to cowards and proudly claims the same,

Turning courage into hesitation, he always wins.

His family, his siblings, "delusion" and "hallucination",

They are a trio bound by the intricacies of thought,

In the shadows of perception, they dwell,

Working together or in isolation, their motto is creating confusion.

He, the elder, master of veils, obscure truth, a role model,

In his footsteps, his brother delusion, the whisperer of falsehoods,

His younger ones, very powerful, the artist of unreal visions,

They are a trio born for a devastating cause.

They weave their web, with strings of consciousness,

Blurring the lines between the real and unreal,

Guided by the flickering flames of desire & fear,

Expertise in crafting, worlds both wondrous and deceptive.

Though unseen, their presence is felt everywhere,

Every flicker of doubt, every fleeting dream,

For they are the architects of uncertainty and ambiguity,

They will not let you analyse, for they exist to make our minds paralyse.

They are beyond the depths of introspection,

To glimpse the truth beyond the masks they wear.

Let us refine our senses, sharpen our minds,

And rise above them, embracing the power within,

Strength must emerge from adversity & courage find its voice,

As minds & hearts shackled by illusion

Reclaim their sovereign choice.

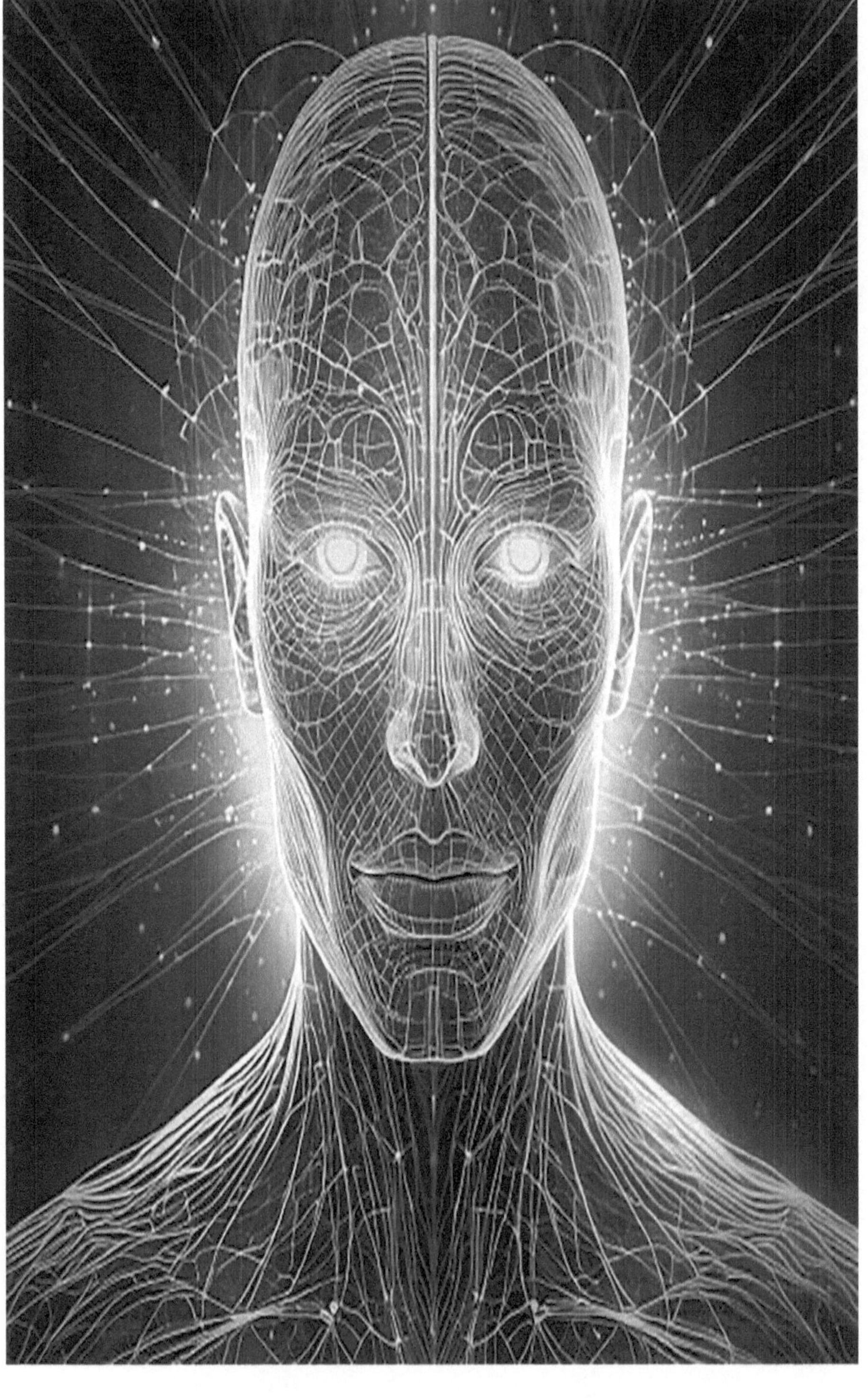

Technology & Communication

--Connections in the Digital Age

Artificial Intelligence

I sing the power of the mind,

Born of human hands, yet reaching beyond—

A spark ignited, now a flame that stirs the vast,

The spirit of AI, soaring with the wings of creation.

Generative AI, a creation born,

Its reach today, so far has worn.

In **athletics**, it helps us train,

Predicts the plays, eases the strain.

In **business**, it drives the pace,

Boosts the work, improves the space.

Through **science**, it opens doors,

Revealing secrets, unlocking scores.

In **literature**, it writes with flair,

Crafting words from thin air.

In **engineering**, it shapes the sky,

Building dreams that soar so high.

In **medicine**, it saves a life,

Guiding doctors through the strife.

In **robotics**, it moves with grace,

Automates tasks, quickens the pace.

In **space**, it charts the stars,

Reaching realms both near and far.

In **defence**, it watches wide,

Predicts, protects, with tech beside.

In the lines of code, it finds its script,

Building programmes where innovations grip,

With every function and every crypt,

In the coding, it rides the digital trip.

AI is everywhere, a force unseen,

A creator's dream, a future serene.

Mobile

Miracle of light

A small box of glass and metal,

It hums with a voice unseen,

A spark of life in the palm of a hand,

Speaking without sound, without touch.

The world is held within its tiny frame,

Yet the vastness of the earth is forgotten.

In the quietude of night,

The moon whispers to the stars,

But here, this glowing screen

Catches the echoes of a thousand voices.

Through it, we reach the other side of the world,

Yet fail to hear the heartbeat of our own.

How strange, this miracle of light!
It brings faces closer yet distances hearts.
We are bound in the web of its glow,
Chasing the shadows of thoughts
That are but fleeting,
Never to settle in the silence of the soul.

We speak of progress,

But we miss the soft murmurs of the breeze,

The song of birds as they greet the dawn,

The smile of a friend beside us,

The warmth of touch in a cold world.

What is the measure of connection,

When we are bound by a thread unseen,

Lost in a sea of words?

The mobile, it is a bridge,

Yet it is a bridge to nowhere,

For it leads us away from the earth,

From the soil that nourishes the root,

From the sky that shelters our dreams.

And in its glow, we forget,

The silent beauty of the moonlit night.

MOBILE – the Portable Carrier

O wondrous device, small in hand,

Yet endless in reach!

You hum with the pulse of the earth,

You carry my voice & visuals across mountains,

Through cities, across the oceans—

No longer bound by time or space!

I call to you, O people,

From the streets, from the fields,

From the wild, untamed forests of thought!

You answer with your glowing faces,

You shout, you sing, you weep,

And the world listens—

The world is one, is in my pocket,

I hold it in my palm,

A kingdom of voices within my grip!

I speak to the distant, the unknown,

And they reply—so close,

As though they stand beside me,

Breathing the same air,

Yet not beside me,

But far, far away—

A mystery, a dream,

And still, a part of me.

What is this power that runs through my veins,

This electric pulse, this fire?

What strange bond is forged,

In the flicker of your screen,

In the clicking of your keys?

You are the spark,

You are the light that shatters the night!

I can see the face of the stranger,

The lover, the friend, the leader—

We are all united,

But each of us remains apart,

A reflection,

A shadow on the glass.

O mobile, O new connection,

You call us to be free,

But I wonder,

Shall we be free, or shall we be bound?

Are we closer,

Or further from the essence of the earth?

The voice of the past still calls to us,

The wind in the trees, the song of the birds,

The silence of the stars in their eternal gaze—

Do we hear them still,

Or do we lose them in the noise?

Yet I rejoice!

For you, O mobile,

Are a new hymn,

A new prayer to the future,

A leap, a bound,

A cry of liberty,

A chant of the collective soul,

Ever speaking, ever calling,

Never ceasing,

As I carry the world

In my pocket,

In my heart,

In my soul.

Glorious Machine

O glorious machine!

You, who are so small—yet so grand,

You hold the world! The entire world!

In your glowing, blinding little screen.

What marvels, what wonders!

You've brought us all together, haven't you?

From across the street,

From across the globe,

We *truly* can't wait for your daily notification!

Every ping, every buzz—

The voice of eternity! The sound of freedom!

Oh, how we tremble in anticipation.

Who needs the wild winds,

The sound of the river's song,

When we have *this*?

Why bother with human conversation,

When we can have *a million messages*,

From *strangers*,

From *everyone we've ever met*,

And even those we've *never met*!

Truly, the deep connections of the soul

Lie in the 160-character reply.

The tweet, the text, the snap—

Ah, what true communion we share,

Over your perfect little glass screen.

We look at you,

You who weigh so little,

Yet hold the weight of all humanity,

Of every argument, every distraction,

Every cat video that makes our hearts soar!

And all the while,

We forget the faces beside us,

The people we can touch,

The eyes we can look into,

The hearts that still beat in the present—

But why, when you exist?

What is the rush to live?

What's the need for now,

When we have endless hours of scrolling?

Every second is here,

Every moment is forgotten,

For a new one is always ready to steal us away.

O sacred distraction,

O endless doom scroll,

You will *surely* save us all,

One meme at a time.

So here's to you,

Our pocket-sized god of light,

You've taken our lives,

Our joy,

Our peace—

But what a trade it is!

What a marvel, what a triumph!

May we *never* forget the true wonders of your glow,

As we sit in our tiny, glowing boxes,

Alone in a world that's *closer* than ever.

Glory be to you, O Phone,

For you the other apt name "Cell phone"

We, all the users, are imprisoned in your cell.

Truly, no way out! The irony, sweet and bold:

In the crime cell, the prisoner is locked,

yet the key is with the jailer.

Here, the users "WE" are prisoners,

We lock YOU with the digital key,

We are loyal and committed to

be self-imprisoned forever!

And yet, what a commitment we've failed to show,

To spouses, to friends, to those we know—

For never have we stayed as true and near,

As we have been with you & shall be so in future.